8 Keys To Accessing the Supernatural

Kimberly Moses

Copyright © 2018 by Kimberly Moses

All rights reserved
Rejoice Essential Publishing
P.O. BOX 512
Effingham, SC 29541

www.republishing.org

All rights reserved. No part of this book may be used or reproduced by any means, graphic, electronic, or mechanical, including photocopying, recording, taping or by any information storage retrieval system without the written permission of the publisher except in the case of brief quotations embodied in critical articles and reviews.

Unless otherwise indicated, Scripture is taken from the King James Version

Visit the author's website at www.prophetessk.org
8 Keys To Accessing The Supernatural/ Kimberly Moses

ISBN-10: 1-946756-20-2
ISBN-13: 978-1-946756-20-6

Library of Congress Control Number: 2018932376

DEDICATION

Tron, you are the reason why this book came into fruition. You were able to see a book out of the series that the Lord gave me at the Glory Conference. I am glad that I listened to you and I know the readers are glad also.

Table Of Contents

Acknowledgment..viii
What Is The Supernatural?...........................1
Is The Supernatural Biblical?.......................8
Demonstration Of The Kingdom................12
Relationship With The Holy Spirit............16
Portals...20
Time...23
Atmosphere...27
Innerman..30
Revelation..32
Triggers..36
Faith Activations...40

ACKNOWLEDGEMENTS

I am thankful to Jesus my Lord and Savior. I Am also thankful for Everyone That Supports This Ministry.

CHAPTER ONE

What Is The Supernatural?

We all heard of the supernatural. There are television shows about this and even radio broadcasts. Many people are afraid of it. Some just don't understand and believe in it, while others don't know how to access it. The fact of the matter is that the supernatural world around us exists. There is another realm outside of the natural one that we interact with on a daily basis.

The supernatural is a force beyond scientific understanding or the laws of nature.[1] Scientists will try to explain a miracle and even discredit God. They will even come up with theories on why something occurred. Sometimes, it's difficult to theorize the supernatural. It's just a force beyond our natural understanding. When most people think of the supernatural, they automatically think demonic. The enemy wants the children of God to be ignorant of this realm.

2 Corinthians 2:11 says, "Lest Satan should get an advantage of us: for we are not ignorant of his devices." The supernatural realm doesn't only belong to the enemy and his kingdom to dominate it. As children of God, we need access to the supernatural realm. If witches, psychics, and the occult can access this realm, why can't the children of the most High God? When we access the supernatural realm, miracles happen. We will go over miracles in detail in the next chapter. Many people may think the enemy

created the supernatural or it originated from him. That is not true. In Exodus 17, Aaron threw down his staff, and it became a serpent. The Pharaoh's magicians were able to copy this. Their staffs turned into serpents as well when they threw them down. Aaron's staff swallowed up the serpents. We can see from this passage that the enemy is a copycat, and he has power, but not as much power as Jehovah.

The supernatural realm is very real. It is so real that once, a witch came into my room. I was asleep on the couch. I felt a hand snatch my soul from my body. I cried out, the hand lost a grip of my soul, and I could feel my soul go back into my body. I opened my eyes and saw a light-skinned lady standing over me. She had dark hair with a long bang covering up her eyebrows. I immediately reacted and went into prayer. After I calmed down, the Holy Spirit gave me her name and her location. I looked this witch up on social media, and she existed. We had no connections whatsoever. I was baffled that she was able to locate me. If I was ignorant of the supernatural, it could've cost me my life. This experience reminded me of how God told Prophet Elisha the secrets that the King spoke in his bedchamber (2 Kings 6:12). God is strategic and always provides great insight.

Before we explore the eight ways of accessing the supernatural, let me share some of my supernatural encounters. I first discovered the supernatural realm as a small child. I could see this little red man everywhere I went. No one could see him except for me. He was just as real to me as my parents and my little sister at the time. I remember talking to this little red man. As a teenager, I could sense an evil presence in my room some nights. I would often awaken to a frightening image of a demonic figure standing over me. The demons that I encountered were tall and dark. Some had piercing red eyes. Many years later, as an adult, I would have many encounters with my Lord and Savior Jesus Christ and the Lord, Almighty.

I remember being discouraged after my first wedding plans didn't go the way I intended. I was hurt and even humiliated. So many people came to attend my wedding ceremony. Many came from out of town. The ceremony was canceled, and I was devastated. I rushed into the bathroom in this tiny villa that my cake decorator found to host the ceremony at the last minute. Inside the bathroom, I saw the face of Jesus Christ on the wall and it disappeared. Seeing His face brought me a sense of comfort.

There were many times I could've gotten into a bad car accident but for some reason, my foot hit the brakes suddenly, I didn't go over in the other lane hitting a car in my blind spot, or I looked up at the right moment after being distracted by my cellphone or by my children in the backseat. There were times when I was ministering on LIVE broadcasts on Periscope, Facebook, YouTube and the breath of God just blew upon me. Everyone on the broadcast attested they felt these winds also. It was so powerful because no windows were open for a draft to come through. No fans were on. No air conditioning was on. There were other times when I could feel the wings of angels brushing up against my skin. I couldn't see them with my natural eyes, but I could feel their feathery wings brushing up against my hands and my arms when I was in worship.

I feel the fire of God on a daily basis. I can feel His presence in various parts of my body. I developed a sensitivity to His presence over the years, so I know where His Glory is manifested. There were times when I needed finances, and I would see a vision about it in prayer and what I saw would get deposited in my account by random sources. I have seen many visions of the sick being healed, and it manifested right before my eyes. Once, a lady came to me asking for prayer for her friend.

Her friend had just had a baby and was in a coma. She never got a chance to see her born child. As I started praying, I saw a vision of her sitting in a wheelchair being pushed outside of the hospital. I told the lady, 'I believe your friend will wake up out of the coma. I can see her going home." That very hour, the lady's friend woke up from the coma.

Just living my daily life, I can hear the voice of God or the enemy. I can feel different spirits in the atmosphere. The list goes on and on. This is what the supernatural looks like in my life. Again, children of God need to know how to have access to the supernatural realm. The Greek word for access is prosagoge.[2] This word means to approach or enter into a place. After having various encounters, I decided to become knowledgeable about this topic. If there is a desire to access the supernatural, then you can. Psalm 107:9 says, "For he satisfieth the longing soul, and filleth the hungry soul with goodness."

CHAPTER TWO

Is The Supernatural Biblical?

Many people who lack knowledge of the supernatural will say it doesn't exist. Hosea 4:6 says, "My people are destroyed for lack of knowledge." As children of God, we need to live the supernatural life. For years, I was a pew warmer. I sat in church with no power. I had no desire for it. I was carnal and consumed only with myself. I wasn't a threat to the enemy's kingdom until I became I serious with the Lord Jesus Christ. Once this happened, the enemy tried to kill me several times. He oppressed me with suicidal thoughts. He told me every day for years how he hated me and was going to kill me. I was bound with anxiety for five years. I got in a horrible car accident after I felt the presence of death and heard the devil tell me that I was going to die that day.

I was fighting against a force that I couldn't always see with my natural eyes, but I was deeply tormented. When I went into a wilderness season where I was very isolated, thousands of miles away from my family, I cried out to Jesus. He manifested himself to me in several trances and visions. Afterwards, He called me as His prophet. I came into the knowledge of His Glory and who He was. My life was never the same. I learned to live a supernatural life and trust God as my source in all things. God provided me a ram in the bush Just as God did for Abraham when he was about to sacrifice his son Isaac (Genesis 22:13). It's supernatural that a ram would get caught in the bush at the right moment.

Let's look at some supernatural occurrences in the bible.

• Jesus fed the five thousand (Matthew 14:13-21)

• He walked on water (Matthew 14:22-33)

• He raised Lazarus from the dead (John 11:38-44);

• He cast out a legion (around six thousand) of demons from a man (Luke 8:26-39)

• Apostle Peter's shadow healed the sick (Acts 5:15)

• Elijah prayed down fire from the sky (1 Kings 18:38)

8 Keys To Accessing The Supernatural

- Elisha caused an axe head to float (2 Kings 6)

- An angel shut the mouth of the lions when Daniel was throw in their den (Daniel 6)

- Abraham and Sarah conceived a child at an old age (Genesis 21)

- Moses parted the Red Sea (Exodus 14)

- Manna came from heaven daily to feed the children of the Israelites (Exodus 16)

- God orchestrated a big fish to swallow up Jonah (Jonah 1:17)

- The virgin birth (Luke 1:26-38)

- Jesus turned water into wine (John 2:1-11)

Now put yourself in this category. What are some supernatural occurrences in your life? Have you witnessed any? Do you want to know more about accessing the supernatural?

CHAPTER THREE

Demonstration Of The Kingdom

God is a supernatural God, and He is a spirit. John 4:24 says, "God is a Spirit: and they that worship him must worship him in spirit and in truth." The next verse also confirms that God is a spirit. 2 Corinthians 3:17 says, "Now the Lord is that Spirit: and where the Spirit of the Lord is, there is liberty." God will supersede our natural. He will cause money to appear in our bank accounts miraculously. He sends angels to protect us. He will sustain us in dry seasons. He will multiply the little that we may have and cause an abundance in our lives. God demonstrated His supernatural ability when He created the foundation of the world by just speaking commands. It all started out with His spirit hovering over waters (Genesis 1). God expects us to demonstrate His kingdom. Demonstrating the kingdom is supernatural.

The kingdom is God's way of doing things. It is having a different mindset to operate in the supernatural realm. It's all about accessing our birthright as children of God (Galatians 3:26; Romans 8:16; Ephesians 1:5; John 1:12) and walking in the authority that Jesus Christ gave us (Mark 3:15; Matthew 10:1; Mark 6:7; Luke 9:1). When we take a close look at Matthew 10:7-8, we see some signs that the kingdom of God has come. When the kingdom comes, the sick will get healed, the lepers will get cleansed, the dead will get raised, and demons will get cast out.

We are called to demonstrate the kingdom of God. Every time I minister, something supernatural occurs. Prophecy comes forth, the sick are healed, and people are delivered. This is just normal to me. Signs and wonders follow. Signs and wonders are supposed to follow those that believe in Jesus Christ. Mark 16:17-18 says, "And these signs shall follow them that believe; In my name shall they cast out devils; they shall speak with new tongues; They shall take up serpents; and if they drink any deadly thing, it shall not hurt them; they shall lay hands on the sick, and they shall recover." Prophecy is supernatural because I am speaking the oracles of God. An unbeliever will know that God is real when the matters of their heart are revealed if they were to walk into the midst of a group of people prophesying (1 Corinthians 14:24-25). When we received salvation, it became our duty to share our faith with others. This is part of the great commission (Matthew 28:16-20).

You can demonstrate the kingdom as well. There has to be a desire for it. Keep on stirring up that spiritual hunger by asking, seeking, and knocking. Luke 11:9-10 says, "And I say unto you: Ask, and it shall be given to you; seek, and ye shall find; knock, and it shall be opened unto you. For every one that asketh receiveth; and he that seeketh findeth; and to him that knocketh it shall be opened."

CHAPTER FOUR

Relationship With The Holy Spirit

The first key to accessing the supernatural is having a relationship with the Holy Spirit. Any access to the supernatural outside of the Holy Spirit is illegal access. The more time we spend with the Lord, the more information we will receive. The more time I spend with the Lord, the more accurate I am in the prophetic. I will receive names, address, dates, and a plethora of information. The key to prophetic accuracy is intimacy with the Holy Spirit. I don't have to seek a psychic for information. This is what King Saul did. First, he banned all witches from the land, and near his death, he sought a witch for information (1 Samuel 28). He was desperate. He had no relationship with God. He loved people more than he loved God. He failed to follow the instructions the Lord gave him because he was afraid of the people (1 Samuel 15). He was the people's king and not God's King.

God can trust my heart and give me access to hidden information. It's like a husband getting to know his wife. They have to spend a lot of time together and learn each other for a lifetime. Our relationship with God is the most important relationship we will ever have. In your tough times, He will be there. When everyone rejects you, He will be right there. I have discovered in deep pain that the Holy Spirit is my comforter.

When I was battling depression, His spirit came into my room. I could feel His fire all over me, and it brought me such a great comfort.

Let's examine the following scriptures. John 14: 16-18 says, "And I will pray the Father, and he shall give you another Comforter, that he may abide with you for ever; Even the Spirit of truth; whom the world cannot receive, because it seeth him not, neither knoweth him: but ye know him; for he dwelleth with you, and shall be in you. I will not leave you comfortless: I will come to you." Notice that Jesus said that the Holy Spirit would abide in us, dwell with us, and be in us. These are powerful verses to show that the Holy Spirit is the legal way of accessing the supernatural realm. Whenever we go through God, there are no strings attached compared to accessing the supernatural through the devil.

There are always strings attached when it comes to the enemy. He will give you power, fame, and riches all for your soul, blood sacrifices, curses on family, and the list goes on and on. He tried to tempt Jesus in the wilderness in Luke 4 with the lust of the flesh, lust of the eye, and the pride of life. However, his schemes did not prosper. Jesus told Satan that he would never worship him but worship only God. Jesus came to destroy the works of the devil (Acts 10:38).

CHAPTER FIVE

Portals

The second key to accessing the supernatural are portals. A portal is a door or entrance.[3] Some people may argue and say portals aren't biblical. However, they are, because doors and gates are mentioned in the bible several times. Psalm 24:9 and Revelation 3:20 are two examples out of many. Certain areas are known for the presence of God or angelic visitations. I visited a place called Moravian Falls, North Carolina, in March 2017. The presence of God was strong in the mountain tops in this small town. It was very serene, and the peace of God was strong. Many people have testified that they had angelic encounters in this small town. When I looked up the history on Moravian Falls, the founding people of this town got together and prayed for a very long time. Since they established an atmosphere of prayer, it was easy to have a portal to heaven. It was easy for God to manifest His presence in this small town.

The Wailing Wall in Jerusalem is known to have a strong presence of the Lord. An old friend of mine told me that as soon as he got close to the wall, he started weeping because the presence of God was so strong. Many people bring their prayer requests and pray at this wall. Prayer is vital in establishing portals into the supernatural. In my old living room in my old apartment, I received several visitations from Jesus Christ. I prayed and worshipped the Lord for hours in my old living room. I was blessed to have the Lord respond to my spiritual hunger. We will discuss certain things we can do later in this book to get a response from heaven. In Genesis 28, Jacob found a portal to heaven. He had a dream of angels ascending and descending. He even saw the Lord at the top of this ladder. He named this place Bethel, which means the house of God.

Just as there are good portals, there are also demonic portals. Certain things we do will allow the enemy access to our lives. The enemy comes in when we sin, watch or listen to certain things. As a teenager, I had demonic visitations almost nightly. I was horrified. It took me receiving salvation, getting baptized, and studying the word of God for these visitations to stop. I also had to live uprightly before God and make sure the demonic portals were closed in my life.

CHAPTER SIX

Time

Time is the third key to accessing the supernatural. The Greek word for time can be defined in Chronos[4] and Kairos[5]. Chronos is a sequence of events that we use on a daily basis such as second, minute, hour, day, month, and year. It's time in chronological order. Kairos is an opportune moment or the right time. God operates on Kairos moments where He can bypass Chronos time. Certain festivals in the bible were known to have a visitation from God. These include Yom Kippur and Rosh Hashanah together (Lev. 23:24-32), or Feasts of Tabernacles (Lev. 23:34-36). These were God's appointed time or holy convocation days (Leviticus 23:2).

We have to make sure that we are in alignment with God's will. We have to sacrifice our time for His. Jesus wept over Jerusalem because they missed their Kairos moment. They missed their visitation from the Lord. Luke 19:44 says, "And shall lay thee even with the ground, and thy children within thee; and they shall not leave in thee one stone upon another; because thou knewest not the time of thy visitation." Don't miss your hour of visitation! Mark 1:15 gives an example of a Kairos moment. When Jesus went forth preaching after John the Baptist's imprisonment, He said, "The time is fulfilled."

Prophetic people are sensitive to time. They wake up at certain hours to pray and be watchmen on the wall. The bible mentions certain watches or certain hours of the day when people prayed. It's important that we apply the same principles to obtain total victory in every area of our lives. Let's examine the following scriptures.

Lamentations 2:19 says, "Arise, cry out in the night: in the beginning of the watches pour out thine heart like water before the face of the Lord: lift up thy hands toward him for the life of thy young children, that faint for hunger in the top of every street."

Judges 7:19 says, "So Gideon, and the hundred men that were with him, came unto the outside of the camp in the beginning of the middle watch; and they had but newly set the watch: and they blew the trumpets, and brake the pitchers that were in their hands."

Exodus 14:24 says, "And it came to pass, that in the morning watch the LORD looked unto the host of the Egyptians through the pillar of fire and of the cloud, and troubled the host of the Egyptians,"

1 Samuel 11:11 says, "And it was so on the morrow, that Saul put the people in three companies; and they came into the midst of the host in the morning watch, and slew the Ammonites until the heat of the day: and it came to pass, that they which remained were scattered, so that two of them were not left together."

Notice the different watches in these scriptures. Beginning of the watches (Lamentations 2:19), the middle watch (Judges 7:19), and the morning watch (Exodus 14:24; 1 Samuel 11:11). The Lord gave me a set time to pray one season and His presence would come strong in my room every day. Establish a time in your life where you can have total devotion to God.

CHAPTER SEVEN

Atmosphere

The fourth key to accessing the supernatural is atmospheres. Certain atmospheres attract the supernatural. This can work both for God and the enemy. Years ago, I visited Peru, and a witch doctor came to my hotel. He was the town's shaman. I was on a medical internship and I wasn't saved at the time. He gathered all the medical students and offered us an opportunity to make contact with our ancestors. He told us about leaves called Chacruna so we could have outer body experiences. Immediately, an eerie feeling came over me. This feeling reminded me of how I felt as a teenager when a demonic presence came into my room. I knew it was wrong, so I denied it. I didn't participate in the shaman's ritual. The enemy will use hallucinogenic drugs and certain music to allow demons to enter the minds and bodies of people.

Whenever we establish prayer, worship, meditation, and total devotion to the Lord, we attract an atmosphere for His presence to dwell. We know that God is everywhere, but His presence, His Glory doesn't manifest equally everywhere. We can see this when the ark of the covenant was taken out of Israel (1 Samuel 4). Eli's daughter-in-law named her son Ichabod because the Glory of the Lord departed. God's presence will manifest in a place where he isn't grieved. We are told not to grieve the Holy Spirit (Ephesians 4).

God wants us to present our bodies as a living sacrifice (Romans 12:1). We have to practice living sacrificially by denying carnality. We can't do everything the world is doing (John

17:16). Whenever we go to certain churches or gatherings, the presence of God will surely manifest. In God's presence is healing, restoration, and breakthrough. His riches are in the Glory (Philippians 4:19). In Luke 2, there was a prophetess named Ana. She set the atmosphere with worship and fasting day and night. When Simeon, a devout man, walked into the atmosphere, he was able to prophesy and recognize the Messiah when Mary and Joseph walked into the temple. This is why atmospheres are so vital in accessing the supernatural. I love to play worship music throughout my house as a way of welcoming the Lord's presence.

CHAPTER EIGHT

Inner Man

The fifth key to accessing the supernatural is the inner man. I heard about the inner man one day in prayer. This is our temple which is the temple of the Holy Spirit. Where we go, we should take the Lord with us. Where our feet tread, it's like God is treading new territories with us. Ephesians 3:16 says, "That he would grant you, according to the riches of his glory, to be strengthened with might by his Spirit in the inner man;" God wants to be strong in us, and we will be strengthened by His spirit. When our inner man is strengthened, we can manifest the kingdom of God on a higher dimension.

Ephesians 3:19 says, "And to know the love of Christ, which passeth knowledge, that ye might be filled with all the fulness of God." God wants us to be full of him so that we can pour out unto others. We need to be so saturated with God's presence that whenever we show up somewhere, lives are changed, and the power of God is demonstrated. This is why the gifts that God placed in our lives aren't for us but others. Whenever I go somewhere, if there is a sick person around me, I can feel an anointing, and I know that God wants me to pray for that person's healing. This is supernatural. I made a decision to yield my inner man and my body for His Glory. Romans 6:13 says, "Neither yield ye your members as instruments of unrighteousness unto sin: but yield yourselves unto God, as those that are alive from the dead, and your members as instruments of righteousness unto God." We need to make sure the Lord dwells in a clean temple and get rid of contaminants such as pride, rebellion, envy, lust, etc.

CHAPTER EIGHT
Revelation

Revelation comes from a divine source, and it's like a lightbulb moment. This is when something is revealed to you for the first time. One day, I was cleaning up my kitchen, and I heard the Lord speak to me. He said, "You lost the art of meditation." He was right, and I got so convicted. I got a revelation of what true meditation was and started applying it to my devotion time unto the Lord. This was very supernatural because as I opened up my bible and started meditating on scriptures, I would feel the fire of God consuming me.

One day, when I was praying, the Glory of God

came into my room and pinned me to the floor. I could only look to the right or left but couldn't move the rest of my body due to His heavy presence. I saw the hand of the Lord come out of my ceiling and he handed me a scepter. He said, "Here is the scepter of righteousness. Teach my people about righteousness." At that time, I had no clue what righteousness was, but after that encounter, there was a download. I knew what righteousness was and wrote a book called "In Right Standing: A Daily Devotional."

I have received many of my books by revelation and even my teaching. It all started with the revelation that the Lord gave me. Whenever we receive revelation, we need to ask God for the interpretation, then apply it so we can get manifestation. Zechariah, the prophet, received revelation when he had eight nighttime visions (Zechariah 1:7-6:15). We can see a pattern where he would ask God what the meaning of this vision was. Then God would send an angel to give the interpretation of the vision. Elisha's servant received revelation when he prayed for his eyes to be opened. His servant realized that there are more fighting with him than against him that day. 2 Kings 6:17 says, "And Elisha prayed, and said, Lord, I pray thee, open his eyes, that he may see. And the Lord opened the eyes of the young man; and he saw: and, behold, the mountain was full of horses and chariots of fire round about Elisha."

Whenever we have a revelation about something, we can then access it supernaturally. Where it used to be hidden, it is now revealed. God wants to give His children revelation because His secrets belong to the righteous (Proverbs 3:32). When I got a revelation of what the word of knowledge was then, I began to operate in it more frequently. One day, I was on the phone with a pastor. All of a sudden, I felt sharp aching fire in my left knee. This made me yell out in pain. I didn't know what this feeling was or why I had it. I felt led to ask the pastor if his left knee hurt and he said yes. He said his knee had bothered him for many years. I stepped out in faith and prayed for his knee. Miraculously, the pain left. A few weeks later, the pastor called me again and testified that his knee was totally healed. Revelation can change your life. It changed mine.

CHAPTER NINE

Triggers

The seventh thing we can do to access the supernatural is by doing certain things. I refer to these things as triggers. Fasting, worship, prayer, and meditation can all get heaven's attention. Daniel fasted and then had an angelic visitation. We can see this in Daniel chapter ten. When I did my first seven days fast, I had a vision of a man sitting in a recliner. He was watching television. Inside the television was a head of a demon mocking him. On both sides of the man were demons. There was one on the left side and another on the right side. They were dancing around the man. It was shocking to see this because the man wasn't aware of their presence. I prayed to God to ask what I was seeing.

Here is the interpretation: Many people are spiritually blinded. They are ignorant of the tricks and schemes of the enemy. The enemy is subconsciously planting seeds to bring destruction, chaos, and confusion to many lives that will eventually take root, but sadly, many people aren't even aware. One way the enemy does this is through social media; that's why it is important to guard what you set before your eyes. The Lord then gave me five prayer tips.

• Pray that you won't be ignorant of the schemes of the enemy

• Pray that you won't be spiritually blinded

• Pray that God will raise up more Godly influences on the media

• Pray that this nation will repent of their wicked

ways

• Pray that you will guard your eye and ear gates

Worship attracts the presence of the Lord and opens up the heavens for supernatural encounters. Prophets in the bible along with the priest had to keep the fire burning on the altar. God was the one who ignited the fire. They weren't allowed to set the fire themselves. This is how Aaron's two sons died because they set strange fire (Leviticus 10). Asaph was a prophet, and his job was to constantly worship before the ark of the covenant (1 Chronicles 16:37). One day as I was worshipping, I started speaking in tongues, and I was able to interpret my own tongues afterward. It was a prophecy about what God wanted to do in my life in that season.

Praying can allow you to access the supernatural. On the day of Pentecost, a group of people was praying in the upper room for days. They were tarrying in prayer, and they received the gift of speaking in tongues (Acts 2). Whenever someone asks me for prayer, I always end up prophesying over them. Prayer is a bridge for prophecy. Remember, there are certain triggers that you can do access the supernatural.

CHAPTER TEN

Faith Activations

The eighth way to access the supernatural is by activating your faith. Faith is the currency of the kingdom of God. Faith is how the kingdom works. The currency of the United States is the dollar. The currency in Mexico is the peso. The most common currency in Europe is the euro. Faith, for a believer, is not an option but a requirement. Hebrews 10:38 says, "Now the just shall live by faith: but if any man draw back, my soul shall have no pleasure in him." I learned on this journey that this is a faith walk. I wrote a book called

"Walk By Faith: A Daily Devotional." This book is full of various trials that I encountered and how I used my faith to overcome. I had to speak to mountains and believe that God was working on my behalf, even though it seemed like nothing was happening.

When my cabinets were bare, I commanded food to fill up the shelves. God made sure that food was in my house shortly after. When I had to pay certain bills and my funds were low, I had to decree that the bills would be paid on time. Month after month, God blessed me financially when I had no secular job but believing Him to sustain me monthly. God always comes through. I had to activate my faith in order to access the supernatural realm. Whenever I pray for someone to get healed, I always tell them to activate their faith by doing something they couldn't do before. Most of the time, it works. They get healed instantly.

Jesus had to activate his faith by commanding

Lazarus to come forth from the dead. Imagine how it must have looked to a carnal person. "This man is speaking to the dead?" Whenever we apply our faith, we might look crazy to the world, but this is the kind of faith that produces miracles. Noah activated his faith when he had an encounter with God. He knew that he was instructed to build an ark. There was no sign of rain, but he stepped out in faith and obeyed the Lord (Genesis 6:22). He was mocked by the onlookers, but he kept on building the ark. He witnessed the supernatural when he and his family were spared from the flood.

Elijah prayed for it to rain. He told Ahab that it was going to rain way before there was any evidence of rain. He even had his servant go search for a cloud. On the seventh time, his servant finally saw a small cloud (1 Kings 18:41-46). It took faith for Elijah to tell Ahab to get up and eat because an abundance of rain was coming. David activated his faith by making prophetic decrees on what was going to happen. He told Goliath that God was going to hand him over.

1 Samuel 17:45-47 says, "Then said David to the Philistine, Thou comest to me with a sword, and with a spear, and with a shield: but I come to thee in the name of the Lord of hosts, the God of the armies of Israel, whom thou hast defied. This day will the Lord deliver thee into mine hand; and I will smite thee, and take thine head from thee; and I will give the carcases of the host of the Philistines this day unto the fowls of the air, and to the wild beasts of the earth; that all the earth may know that there is a God in Israel. And all this assembly shall know that the Lord saveth not with sword and spear: for the battle is the Lord's, and he will give you into our hands."

This is what happened. We can learn from David by activating our faith. It's time to access the supernatural realm. Apply these eight keys that we discussed in this book, and you can always live a supernatural life.

About The Author

Kimberly Moses started off her ministry as Kimberly Hargraves. She is a highly sought after prophetic voice, Intercessor and a prolific author. There is no doubt that she has a global mandate on her life to serve the nations of the world by spreading the Gospel of JesusChrist. She has a quickly expanding worldwide healing and deliveranceministry. Kimberly Moses wears many hats to fulfill the call God has placed on her life as an entrepreneur over several businesses including her own personal brand Rejoice Essentials which promotes the Gospel of Jesus Christ. This brand includes a magazine and anointing oils. She also serves as a life coach and mentor to many women. She is married to Tron and also the loving mother of two wonderful children. Kimberly has dedicated her life to the work of ministry and to serve others under the call God has placed over her life.

Kimberly currently resides in South Carolina. She is a very anointed woman of God who signs, miracles and wonders follow. The miraculous and incessant testimonies attributed to her ministry are incalculable, with many reporting physical and mental healing, financial breakthroughs, debt cancellations and other favorable outcomes. She is known across the globe as a servant who truly labors on behalf of God's people through intercession. God blessed her to start her ministry to help encourage others. God used her pain to reveal her writing ability and to do his work. God blessed her to write about life experiences and give a message of hope to others with broken hearts.

She is the author of The Following:

"Overcoming Difficult Life Experiences with Scriptures and

Prayers"

"Overcoming Emotions with Prayers"

"Daily Prayers That Bring Changes"

"In Right Standing,"

"Obedience Is Key,"

"Prayers That Break The Yoke Of The Enemy: A Book Of Declarations,"

"Prayers That Demolish Demonic Strongholds: A Book Of Declarations,"

"Work Smarter. Not Harder. A Book Of Declarations For The Workforce,"

"Set The Captives Free: A Book Of Deliverance."

"Pray More Challenge"

"Empowering The New Me: Fifty Tips To Becoming A Godly Woman"

"Walk By Faith: A Daily Devotional"

"School Of The Prophets: A Curriculum For Success"

"Conquering The Mind: A Daily Devotional"

You can find more about Kimberly at

www.prophetessk.org. Follow Kimberly on Facebook at https://www.facebook.com/seerprophetesskimberlyhargraves/. Follow Kimberly on Twitter and periscope @ SeerProphetessK.

REFERENCE

1) Supernatural. https://en.oxforddictionaries.com/definition/supernatural. Accessed December 24, 2017.

2) G4318 - prosagōgē - Strong's Greek Lexicon (KJV). Retrieved from https://www.blueletterbible.org//lang/lexicon/lexicon.cfm?Strongs=g4318&t=kjv

3) "Portal." Merriam-Webster.com. Merriam-Webster, n.d. Web. 24 Dec. 2017.

4) G5550 - Chronos - Strong's Greek Lexicon (KJV). Retrieved from https://www.blueletterbible.org//lang/lexicon/lexicon.cfm?Strongs=g5550&t=kjv

5) G2540 - kairos - Strong's Greek Lexicon (KJV). Retrieved from https://www.blueletterbible.org//lang/lexicon/lexicon.cfm?Strongs=g2540&t=kjv

INDEX

A

Abraham, 9

abundance, 13, 42

angels, 11, 13, 33

atmosphere, 7, 27–29

B

bible, 10, 20, 23–24, 32, 38

C

ceremony, 5

children, 2, 5, 44

currency, 40

D

Demonstration, 12

devils, 9, 14, 18

E

enemy, 2, 8, 28, 37

F

faith, 14, 35, 40–43

G

Glory, 6, 9, 28–29, 31

H

heart, 14, 17

Holy, 16

Holy Spirit, 16

I

instruments, 31

intercession, 45

J

Jesus, 9–11, 19, 24, 41

K

Kairos, 23–24

kingdom, 2, 9, 12–15, 30, 40

knowledge, 8–9, 34

L

Lazarus, 42

lust, 19

M

Manna, 11

ministry, 44–45

miracles, 2, 42

Moses, 2, 4, 6, 10–11, 14, 18, 22, 24, 26, 28, 42, 44, 46, 48, 50

N

nations, 37, 44

O

opportuiity, 27

P

portals, 20, 22

power, 3, 8

pray, 21, 24, 26, 31, 37–38, 41

prayer, 3, 6, 21, 30, 39, 45

prophecy, 38–39

prophetic accuracy, 17

prophetic decrees, 42

Prophets, 38

R

relationship, 16–17

revelation, 32–35

S

scriptures, 25

season, 26, 38

servant, 34, 42, 45

spiritual hunger, 21

supernatural, 2–3, 5, 7–11, 13–21, 23, 25, 27, 29, 31–33, 35–43, 45, 47, 49, 51

T

temple, 29–30

V

vision, 6, 33–34

visitations, 21–23

W

worship, 6, 12, 19, 29, 38

www.ingramcontent.com/pod-product-compliance
Lightning Source LLC
Chambersburg PA
CBHW071542080526
44588CB00011B/1760